SALTY BITCHES
Vintage Ladies Talking Trash

ADULT COLORING BOOK

Vintage images are from the British Library on-line collection of public domain images
found at www.flickr.com/photos/britishlibrary
A few selections from the National Gallery of Art public domain images
found at https://images.nga.gov

instagram

Post coloring pages on instagram @colormenaughtybooks
#saltybitches

OTHER BOOKS BY COLOR ME NAUGHTY

AND

RISE AND SHINE
BITCHES

YEAH, NO.

BITCH
DON'T KILL MY VIBE

TIME TO DO SOME
SOUL CRUSHING

NO BRA CLUB

BAD BITCH #1

EXCUSE ME, WHAT LANGUAGE ARE YOU SPEAKING? IT SOUNDS LIKE BULLSHIT.

BASIC BITCH

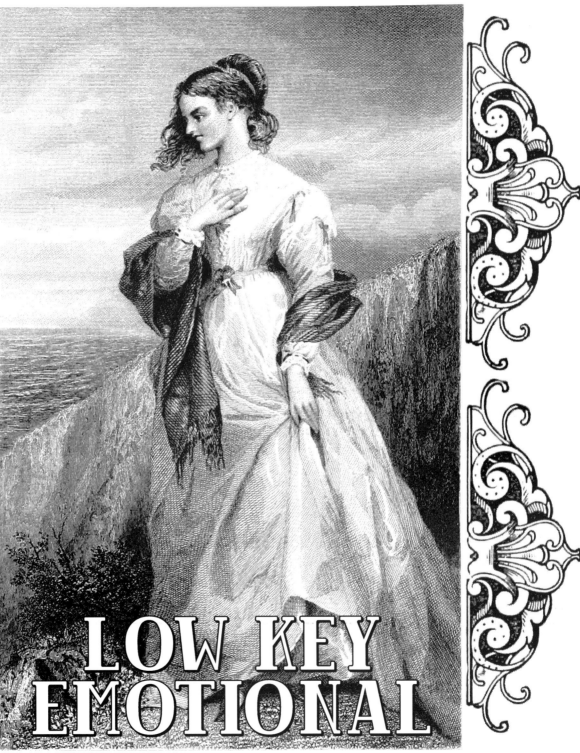

LOW KEY EMOTIONAL

LORD GIVE ME THE STRENGTH TO TOLERATE THIS FAKE BITCH

HATERS
GONNA
HATE

HOLD ON, LET ME OVERTHINK THIS.

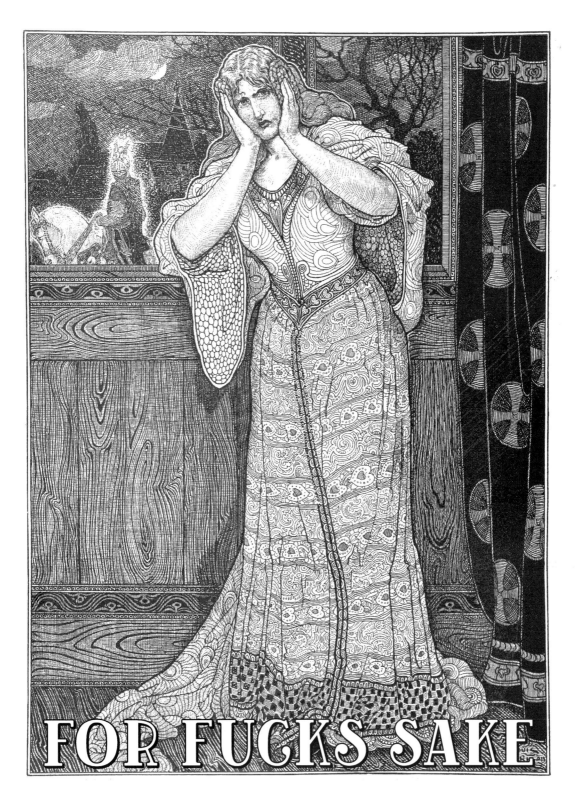

FOR FUCKS SAKE

I AM A RAY OF
FUCKING SUNSHINE

HOT MESS

I AM GOING TO ACT LIKE
I DID NOT SEE THAT SHIT

ZERO FUCKING SELFIE CONTROL

YOU COULDN'T HANDLE
ME EVEN IF I CAME
WITH INSTRUCTIONS.

TRASH TALKING BECKY

THIS IS MY HAPPY FACE

I AM A DELICATE FUCKING FLOWER

EXHALE THE
BULLSHIT

OH ARE YOU TALKING TO ME? I THOUGHT YOU ONLY SPOKE BEHIND MY BACK.

I'M JUST SAYING

I DON'T HAVE A TEMPER.
I HAVE A QUICK
REACTION TO BULLSHIT.

DON'T MAKE
ME FLIP MY
BITCH SWITCH

LIFE ISN'T PERFECT BUT YOUR OUTFIT CAN BE

F B

OMNEM IN HOMINE VENVSTATEM MORS ABOLET.

EFF THAT

I'LL ALLOW IT

Dessiné par Le Prince Peintre du Roi   Gravé par Demarteau

I WOKE UP LIKE THIS

JE SUIS UNE FEMME
SAUVAGE

I CAN
BUT I WON'T

DEAD INSIDE

THANKS, I HATE IT

Lady Jane Grey.

SMASH THE PATRIARCHY

CALM YOUR TITS

GET IT GIRL

KINDLY GO
FUCK YOURSELF

EXCUSE YOU

SHHH, NO ONE CARES

YA BASIC

EAT A BAG OF DICKS

ZERO FUCKS

I MAY BE A BITCH BUT
AT LEAST I'M HONEST

FUCK YOU AND THE HORSE YOU RODE IN ON

BITCH, PLEASE...

UGH
I CAN'T EVEN

STONE COLD BITCH

YAS QUEEN

Made in the USA
Monee, IL
08 December 2019